SCI-FI TE

WHAT WOULD IT TAKE TO MAKE A HOVERBOARD?

BY ANITA NAHTA AMIN

CAPSTONE PRESS
a capstone imprint

Capstone Captivate is published by Capstone Press, an imprint of Capstone.
1710 Roe Crest Drive
North Mankato, Minnesota 56003
www.capstonepub.com

Library of Congress Cataloging-in-Publication Data
Names: Amin, Anita Nahta, author.
Title: What would it take to make a hoverboard? / by Anita Nahta Amin.
Description: North Mankato, Minnesota : Capstone Press, [2020] | Series:
   Sci-fi tech | Includes index. | Audience: Grades 4-6
Identifiers: LCCN 2019029526 (print) | LCCN 2019029527 (ebook) | ISBN
   9781543591156 (hardcover) | ISBN 9781496665959 (paperback) | ISBN 9781543591231 (ebook)
Subjects: LCSH: Ground-effect machines--Juvenile literature. | Personal
   propulsion units--Juvenile literature. | Technological
   innovations--Juvenile literature. | LCGFT: Instructional and educational
   works.
Classification: LCC TL718 .A45 2020 (print) | LCC TL718 (ebook) | DDC
   629.3/22--dc23
LC record available at https://lccn.loc.gov/2019029526
LC ebook record available at https://lccn.loc.gov/2019029527

Image Credits
AP Images: Jeff Chiu, 6, 28–29, Ryan Remiorz/The Canadian Press, 16; iStockphoto: DaydreamsGirl, 7, ktsimage, 12; Newscom: Jean-Paul Pelissier/Reuters, 19, Lexus/SIPA, 20, Nils Jorgensen/Cover Images, 5; Science Source: Brian Bell, 27; Shutterstock Images: anaken2012, 23, Djomas, cover (boy), Hung Chung Chih, 26, Mark and Anna Photography, 11, Mungkhood Studio, 15, Natsmith1, 21, ranchorunner, 14, Viacheslav Nikolaenko, 24–25, zhao jiankang, cover (background); Wikimedia Commons: Daderot, 9
Design Elements: Shutterstock Images

Editorial Credits
Editor: Arnold Ringstad; Designer: Laura Graphenteen

Printed in the United States of America.
PA99

TABLE OF CONTENTS

WORDS IN BOLD ARE IN THE GLOSSARY.

CHAPTER ONE

FLOATING ON AIR

Imagine going down the street **hovering** just a few inches above the ground. You are standing on a board that has no wheels. You wave to your friends. They float by on their own boards. There is a pond ahead. But you don't have to avoid it. You and your friends simply hover over the water.

Floating through air may seem like magic. Hoverboards are in movies. They appear in books. But they still aren't widely available. Scientists are working on hoverboards. One day the dream of floating on air could come true!

FUN FACT

Hoverboards became famous after they were in the 1989 movie *Back to the Future Part II*.

Fans had a chance to buy the same hoverboard used for *Back to the Future Part II.*

Some real-life hoverboards look like large skateboards.

CHAPTER TWO

WHAT IS A HOVERBOARD?

A hoverboard is a board you stand on. It lifts you off the ground. It looks like a floating skateboard, but it does not have any wheels.

How can the hoverboard float? The board must work against **gravity**. This **force** pulls objects to the ground. For a hoverboard to work, there must be an opposite force pushing the board up.

Earth's gravity pulls objects to the ground.

Today most hoverboards are **prototypes**. These designs show an idea. But they are just test models. They are not finished. Scientists are still experimenting. They are trying different designs and ideas. You can't find real hoverboards in stores yet.

AN EARLY PROTOTYPE

The Hiller Flying Platform was an early hoverboard prototype. It was built in the 1950s for the U.S. military. The rider stood on a round platform. Fans blew air downward. The air moving down pushed the platform up. The rider steered by leaning in different directions. The platform was slow and hard to use. The military soon stopped working on it.

A hoverboard prototype called the Hiller Flying Platform can be seen in a museum.

CHAPTER THREE

HOW WOULD A HOVERBOARD WORK?

Hoverboards need three key things to work. First, they need a way to hover. Second, they need energy to power them. And third, they need a way for the rider to steer.

A board can use strong fans to hover. They blow air downward. This pushes the board up. A board could use **jet engines** in a similar way. The engines point downward. They make a stream of hot gases. The hot gases push the board up.

Helicopters use rotors, devices that work like fans, to fly. A hoverboard could use small fans to hover off the ground.

Superconductors can make objects float in midair. This same idea can be used for hoverboards.

Magnets and electricity could also make the board hover. Magnets push against objects that **repel** them. The magnet doesn't have to touch the repelling object. Running electricity through some materials makes them into powerful magnets. Those materials can be placed into a board. Certain surfaces repel them. This lets the board and rider hover. However, the rider can only travel on a surface that repels magnets. Sheets made of some kinds of metal work for this.

For other hoverboards, the magnets are in the floor. The board contains materials called **superconductors**. The superconductors are cooled to low temperatures. This causes them to repel magnets without touching. The board hovers over the magnets in the floor.

Jet engines use fuel to push airplanes forward. Much smaller engines could make hoverboards work.

Energy is needed to power a board. A lot of energy is needed to lift the weight of a rider. But there isn't much room on the board to store that energy. This creates a challenge for board designers.

Boards with fans or magnets use electricity for energy. Electricity is stored in batteries. A board can fit only small batteries inside. It may run for just a few minutes. Then it needs to recharge.

Hoverboards with jet engines use **jet fuel** for energy. The jet engines heat the fuel and mix it with air. Fuel provides more energy than batteries. But storing and using it can be dangerous. Fuel can catch fire and cause explosions.

Once the board is in the air, the rider has to steer it. Riders steer most hoverboards with their bodies. They simply lean in the direction they want to go. Other boards have handheld controllers. A rider can even use a smartphone to steer.

Smartphones could send messages to a hoverboard.

Inventor Alexandru Duru
made the Omni Hoverboard.
It uses downward-blowing fans.

CHAPTER FOUR

CURRENT HOVERBOARD TECHNOLOGY

Companies are testing a few different models of hoverboards today. These boards use different ways to hover.

One model is the ArcaBoard. It uses 36 small fans. They let the board hover up to 12 inches (30 centimeters) off the ground. The fans are made from aluminum. This is a strong, light metal. Still, the board is much larger and heavier than a skateboard. Batteries power the ArcaBoard. Riders can use a smartphone to steer it.

FUN FACT

The ArcaBoard's fans spin 45,000 times per minute!

Another model is the Flyboard Air. Four powerful jet engines lift it into the air. These engines use fuel from a bag on the rider's back. The rider leans and uses a handheld controller to steer.

The Flyboard Air goes faster and higher than other hoverboards. It can zoom at almost 100 miles (160 kilometers) per hour. It can soar hundreds of feet in the air. But it is dangerous. Riders must train for many hours. They practice over water. They fly low and slow at first. That way crashes are less dangerous.

A HOVERBOARDING RECORD

Franky Zapata invented the Flyboard Air. In 2016, he set a hoverboard world record in France. He made the farthest hoverboard flight. Zapata traveled 7,388 feet (2,252 meters).

Riders must wear protective gear when using the Flyboard Air.

A computer inside the board helps control the Flyboard Air. It can make tiny adjustments to keep the rider steady. It also stops the rider from going too high or too fast.

A pro skateboarder tested the Lexus SLIDE.

Another hoverboard is the Lexus SLIDE. It uses magnets, electricity, and superconductors. The superconductors in the board must be cold to work. People pour a super cold liquid into the board.

The board floats over a narrow track. The track has magnets in it. The superconductors repel the magnets without touching them. This holds the board in the air. The rider leans to steer and balance. After about ten minutes, the board warms up. It stops working. More cold liquid is needed to cool it down again.

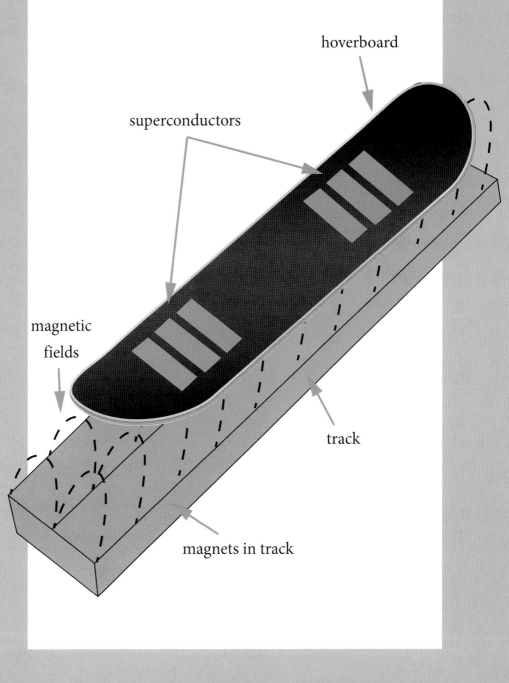

CHAPTER FIVE

WHAT TECHNOLOGY IS NEEDED?

Hoverboards are getting better. But there are still challenges to overcome.

One challenge involves energy. Hoverboards have limited space for batteries. The batteries must be small. This means they run out quickly. Most boards today can only float for a few minutes. Better batteries will allow boards to store more energy. They will be able to float faster and farther.

Another challenge has to do with weight. Lifting more weight takes more energy. A heavier board or rider uses up energy faster. Finding lighter materials for the boards, batteries, and fans will help.

Scientists are working on making better batteries.

Another challenge is control. Riding a hoverboard isn't easy. It can take hours of practice. Staying balanced is harder than on a skateboard. A skateboard has four wheels on the hard ground under it. But a hoverboard doesn't have this to help the rider stay balanced. It's harder to keep steady in the air.

FUN FACT

Hoverboards are much heavier than skateboards. The ArcaBoard weighs 180 pounds (82 kilograms). Regular skateboards weigh up to 10 pounds (4.5 kg).

Balancing is hard on a skateboard. It will be even tougher on a hoverboard.

Steering is tricky. Moving your body or tilting your phone to steer the board takes skill. This is tough on hoverboards that float near the ground. But it is even harder on high-flying boards such as the Flyboard Air. Computers can help control hoverboards and keep them stable. Researchers are working on even better ways for riders to control hoverboards. This will be important to keep riders comfortable and safe.

Some trains use magnets to float above tracks.

CHAPTER SIX

WHAT COULD THE FUTURE LOOK LIKE?

The future of hoverboards is bright. Scientists are learning more about using magnets and fans to keep boards in the air. They are also finding new ways to make things hover. One way uses sound. It has hundreds of tiny speakers. These send out strong sound waves. The force of this sound can lift small objects. In one test, scientists lifted a Styrofoam ball 0.62 inches (16 millimeters) wide. They are working on lifting larger objects.

Scientists tested how small objects might hover using a speaker.

People are also thinking about new ways to use hoverboards. Could they rescue people from natural disasters? Will hoverboarding be a new sport? Will people float along city sidewalks to school or work? The future is full of possibilities.

An engineer tested a magnetic hoverboard on a special metal surface.

There is still a lot of work to do. But scientists are making important steps. Today hoverboards are looking less like science fiction and more like science fact. Perhaps one day you'll glide from place to place on your own hoverboard!

GLOSSARY

force (FORSS)—a push or pull on an object

gravity (GRA-vuh-tee)—a force that pulls objects together; gravity pulls objects down toward the center of Earth

hover (HUV-er)—to float above the ground in midair

jet engine (JET EN-jin)—an engine that burns fuel and shoots out hot gas to push something upward or forward

jet fuel (JET FYOO-uhl)—a chemical mixture that is used to power jet engines

prototype (PRO-toh-tipe)—an early model of a product not yet ready for the public

repel (re-PEHL)—to push something away

superconductor (SOOP-er-con-duk-ter)—a material that pushes strongly against magnets when it is very cold

READ MORE

Rake, Jody S. *What Is Force?* North Mankato, MN: Capstone Press, 2019.

Royston, Angela. *All about Magnetism*. Chicago: Heinemann-Raintree, 2016.

Royston, Angela. *Race That Bike!: Forces in Vehicles.* Chicago: Heinemann-Raintree, 2016.

INTERNET SITES

ArcaBoard
http://www.arcaspace.com/en/arcaboard.htm

The Hendo Hoverboard
https://hendohover.com/the-hendo-hoverboard/

Smithsonian National Air and Space Museum
http://howthingsfly.si.edu/

INDEX